Battered Secrets: <u>*MEN*</u> of Domestic Violence

By
Elva "Precious Love" Thompson

Esquire Publications
P. O. Box 241
Morrow, GA 30260

Esquire Publications
P. O. Box 241
Morrow, GA 30260
www.esquirepublications.com

"Battered Secrets: _MEN_ of Domestic Violence"

Copyright © 2010 by Elva Thompson

This book is a work of nonfiction. All rights reserved. No part of this book may be reproduced or transmitted in any form or by any means, electronic or mechanical, including photocopying and recording, or by any information storage and retrieval system, without permission in writing from the publisher.

Library of Congress Cataloging-in-Publication Data

Library of Congress Control Number: 2010923300

ISBN: 9780982669044

Printed in the United States of America

Acknowledgements

To ALL the brave men that came forth and shared their stories, I commend you and I thank you for allowing me the opportunity to write about your amazing journey.

ABUSE IS **_NEVER_** OKAY
IF YOU OR SOMEONE YOU KNOW IS A VICTIM OF DOMESTIC ABUSE, IMMEDIATELY CALL 911 OR YOUR LOCAL DOMESTIC ABUSE HELPLINE

**1-888-7HELPLINE
(1-888-743-5754)**

THE ABUSE **STOPS** HERE!

www.preciousheartsfoundation.org

"Battered Secrets: _MEN_ of Domestic Violence"

Psalm 127:4-5

As arrows are in the hand of a mighty man; so are children of the youth. Happy is the man that hath his quiver full of them: they shall not be ashamed, but they shall speak with the enemies in the gate.

Table of Contents

<u>Chapter I</u>
Fred Anderson...Page 1

<u>Chapter II</u>
John M..Page 9

<u>Chapter III</u>
Jerry Miranda..Page 15

<u>Chapter IV</u>
Anthony S...Page 22

<u>Chapter V</u>
Jason R...Page 26

<u>Chapter VI</u>
Christopher S..Page 30

<u>Chapter VII</u>
Brian C...Page 34

<u>Chapter VIII</u>
James A..Page 41

<u>Chapter IX</u>
Michael B..Page 46

<u>Chapter X</u>
Marshawn H...Page 53

Elva "Precious Love" Thompson

Chapter *I*

Fred Anderson – 39, Los Angeles, CA
Telecommunications Representative
Separated / Divorce pending
4 Children

"Today, I am on the road to recovery"...**the words conveyed to me from that of Fred Anderson, a 39-year-old telecommunications representative, who wishes to remain anonymous for legality matters. Fred was a victim of domestic violence for a period of 12 years duration at the hands of his soon-to-be ex-wife. He has four children, 3 boys, and 1 girl with his estranged wife. Fred just obtained contact with his children after removing himself from his abusive environment just a little under 2 years ago.**

I knew the kids were going to be missing me. I was the one that would spend time and play with them when I came home from work. I took them to the park and pushed them on the slides and helped them when they wanted to ride their bikes. I was part of their lives. To leave them was a risk I had to take. They were in the middle of my marriage. They were the reason why I stayed for so long in my

Battered Secrets: *MEN* of Domestic Violence

marriage. My wife knew that the kids would always bring me back home when I had left several times before because of something that was thrown at me or for the verbal abuse I had to face. I believe that if I worked hard and tried to provide for the families needs, some how, things might change...It was in the summer of 1996 when my wife and I first met. We started talking over the phone and decided to start dating.

During courtship, we had a few problems in the relationship, but I loved her so much, I wanted to make things work. We were married six months later. After we finally married, she said she wanted an annulment. I have always given the option to try to make the marriage work so we went to marriage counseling in 2000. The counselor told us that I was too passive and my wife was too aggressive.

He stated such because on our way to counseling, riding in the car, for no apparent reason, she would attack me by hitting me on my arm and chest. When I told her to stop, she would keep hitting me until I hit her back. The counselor advised my wife to stop hitting me because it was very abusive behavior. After that session, she refused to follow up therapy because in her own words, "I believe therapy is

Elva "Precious Love" Thompson

swaying your way." Needless to say, we never returned to therapy as a couple and the abuse continued along with objects being thrown at me. At one point, she even threw a dirty diaper at me because she said that I deserved it. One time, when I mentioned about not wanting her sister, who was a bad influence by drinking and smoking in front of my kids living with us, she attacked me by holding me down and choking my neck.

Another incident occurred when I purchased an iPod without her approval, she beat me with a fly swatter on my back. She even went as far as to steal my car from my work place while I was inside. She drove it to a far off lot and then proceeded to smoke in it and spread the ashes all over the dashboard, knowing that I have sinus problems and cigarette smell effects me.

That same night, she abused me by hitting me on the legs rapidly and repeatedly while I was trying to sleep and once in the groin. It was around 3am and I did not call the police. I was scared that she would prevent me from calling because of how abusive the moment was. She told me that she abused me that night because I took our son to church when she did not want to take him. She abused me until 7am. As days went by, she was breaking me down

Battered Secrets: *MEN* of Domestic Violence

day in and day out until finally, I reacted by throwing a bowl of salad on her, but some of the salad accidentally got on my son. She then attacked me by scratching my arms up. That led to restraining orders on both sides. My second one on her, but the first one I had removed because she refused me my kids if I had not. I have never felt that angry before, so I decided to go back to therapy by myself where I was diagnosed with depression and having suicidal thoughts with low self worth. I was therefore prescribed antidepressant drugs and I was taking sleeping pills because I had difficulty falling to sleep because of stress.

Shortly after, we filed for separation. After 5 months of separation, my daughter was born and I still wanted to make the marriage work, so we got back together. I did not want to lose my family. I still loved my wife and I wanted to be with my kids, so I put up with the abuse. I have always wanted to be there with my wife because I wanted my kids to see a person that was not into drinking and smoking, but into a better life. I have never come from an abusive household. During my childhood, I grew up with my aunt, who is a respected churchgoer and choir director until I moved in to live with my mother, a CNA nurse when I got into my teen years. However, my wife has grown up in an abusive household where she

Elva "Precious Love" Thompson

has been beaten heavily by her parents with objects and her mother would not let her or her siblings go to school until their bruises went away. She was even sexually abused by her father, a guard at the penitentiary.

Later in the years, the abuse never stopped, so I began to spend more time at work and less time at home. Then on June 29, 2007, I left my wife after a little over 10 years of marriage, living in hell. My job then transferred me to California. My ex-wife never at any point in her life ever admitted that she had ever abused me, even when I had a police report and went to court and filed a restraining order against her. Not once did she admit that anything was wrong with her abuse. So, in my mind, if she abused me, it was like it did not happen in her mind and I can be abused and she would never admit it. My kids did not like how my wife talked to them and when my son finally said to her that he was scared of her, she changed a little bit.
I was hoping that she would somewhat see what she was doing to the kids. My son, who is 10 years old now, always told me, "Daddy, I don't want you to go." My wife would even quiz the kids on if I should stay or go.

Battered Secrets: *MEN* of Domestic Violence

After I left, my wife wanted to pay me back for leaving so she told my kids that they cannot talk to me and always changed the subject when the kids would wonder where I was or what I was doing. My son had to go to therapy because he had a hard time realizing his dad was gone, and then all the kids went into therapy. After a while, the therapist spoke to my wife and said that she needed to let my kids talk to me. A week before Christmas, I gave her my number so I can talk to the kids, as I do not have a direct number for them. I have to talk to my wife and ask permission to have them call me.

At Christmas, I never sent my kids a gift, just a card. I believe that if I were to send a gift, they would not receive it or be allowed to accept a gift from me. I had forewarned my soon-to-be ex-wife that I was going to leave if she did not stop the abuse, so here I am now leaving her years later. I tried marriage counseling. I tried to show her love and affection. Neither attempts worked. This was the only thing that worked. Leaving gave me freedom from abuse.

I asked Fred what he has learned from this experience: I married my wife because not what God wanted for me, but what I wanted for myself. I never thought that the evil of life would put me where I am today. What I have learned from the experience is that

Elva "Precious Love" Thompson

making choices in life is based on self-sacrifice, based on the ability to have a covenant relationship with one another. Making a relationship work takes two parts, the giving and the taking. The knowledge of your mate is important in knowing how to love and be loved.

I asked Fred how was life for him today: June 29, 2007, the day of remembrance of my goal of recovery, the day I started a change for my life. Living the life I did before June 29, 2007 was a life of anguish and despair. Looking back has made me open my eyes to life in a completely different way. I am so glad I am alive today and feel better because the changes I have made by the help of the Almighty God.

Today, I am happy and feel better than I have before because God changed my life around. Going through the struggles I have been through, there must be a God because what I have experienced and felt in the past has made me feel that I am alive for a reason. I have accomplished a victory of recovery through Christ that I have never felt before until now. Antidepressant drugs - overcome, sleeping pills - no longer have to take, suicide - no more! I read and concentrate on the Bible before going to bed. I have a reason for living. I am a child of God, wonderfully made, not to be hit.

Battered Secrets: *MEN* of Domestic Violence

Fred Anderson has involved himself back into church where he reestablished his relationship with Jesus Christ. He has filed for divorce along with visitation to begin spending time with his children.

Chapter *II*

John M. – 52, Charleston, WV
Businessman

"I believe many men suffer like I did for years and when they finally take all they can, they strike back, sometimes with deadly consequences. With a court system that sides with females when it comes to kids, men stay in relationships that are very damaging to them in order to maintain contact with their children. We cannot solve the problem of domestic violence if we pretend that women are always the victim and men are always the abusers. There are some very bad men and there are also some very bad women..." **The words spoken of a formerly abused 52-year-old father and businessman. In 1993, John was married to his second wife, with whom he bore one son. Shortly afterwards, he became aware that he was married to a woman who was bipolar and a heavy drinker, who was verbally abusive to him, as well as his three other children from a previous marriage. According to John, she was physically abusive early on with a violent temper, like when she put her fist through the door of their home just six months into the marriage.** Each time I would try

Battered Secrets: *MEN* of Domestic Violence

to separate myself from her; she would proclaim that she was pregnant. Her violent outbursts were intermittent with times where she was very fun and nice to be around, but you never knew which "face" would show up.

During one of the times that she was on a high note, I told her I could not stay married unless she got counseling and went to a doctor for the mood disorder. She told me at that time that it ran in the family and that she had been on medication before. We went to a psychiatrist, and after several trials, got on a medication that seemed to end the nightmare. The doctor told her that whatever she did, she should not get pregnant because of the medication that she was on.

I knew that I did not want to have children with her, so I scheduled a vasectomy, which she pressured me into canceling and then became pregnant. The doctor discontinued seeing her because she had not followed his instructions. I wept, knowing we would go through the ups and downs all over again. Things got worse and worse as she could not be on medication because of the pregnancy and she was going through the changes related to the pregnancy. She would get very angry, shout, curse, swear, and belittle the kids and myself in an attempt to make us feel sorry for her.

Elva "Precious Love" Thompson

Over a period of time, she broke almost every door stop in the house when angry by throwing the doors open and or slamming them. I would try to go to the bathroom for solitude and she would use a coat hanger to open the locked door. I would try to turn off the lights in the bedroom and she would turn the lights directly into my eyes and get on top of me in a straddling position to try to elicit an argument. She would slap, scratch, gouge, and threaten to kill me if I left her. She would set the kids up and try to get them into trouble and set a different standard for her son by a previous marriage than she set for my kids.

As soon as her son would go back to his father, she would say it was time to get tough on the kids. She got bit by one of the pet gerbils' and took a shovel and smashed it right in front of the kids. She hit and whipped her horse when it did not do what she thought it should. There were stray cats in the barn with several babies, she tried to poison them and almost killed our pet cats in the process. She then instructed my twin boys to stomp on the baby cats to kill them all because she didn't like to step in cat manure.

One day, there was a stray dog on the porch that would not leave, so she had the boys shoot the dog with a BB gun. When I found

Battered Secrets: *MEN* of Domestic Violence

them on the porch, I asked what was going on and she said she wanted to get rid of the dog. I found blood on the dog where the BB's had hit and reprimanded my boys. I then loaded the dog on the back of a Mule, which is a 4-wheel utility farm machine and took it down the road to let it go.

Another incident was after lunch when I failed to tell her the meal was good and she exploded, saying that she had to *"do it all and got no appreciation."* She started throwing dishes around in the sink and then threw a Tupperware bowl at my daughter as she came through the kitchen. One time, I was washing my hands in the sink and splashed water on the mirror. Before I had time to wipe it off, she was cursing me and yelling about how inconsiderate I was. When I tried to walk away, she grabbed me and threw me into a door, pulling a muscle in my side. I went to the doctor the next day and made a report, however, the doctor never filed the report. It was so bad that I decided to tape one of the arguments because no one believes that women can be so abusive and violent. She found out that I had tapes, which was hidden in my office desk drawer and she broke the lock and destroyed the tapes. I made sure to show my business partner scratches and gouges she did to me on more than

Elva "Precious Love" Thompson

one occasion. Some of the injuries lasted more than a week because of how she would dig in my skin with her fingernails and gouge me.

The last straw came when she got drunk on a vacation with my college roommate, his wife, and all of our children. She went into a fury in front of everyone and then put our son, about 7 years of age at the time, in a car and drove 5 hours in a drunken rage. We had a home in two different states, so I went to one of them to get away from her and sent her a certified letter documenting some of the incidents that have occurred and told her that if she did not quit drinking, then I would not stay in the marriage. In return, she took the letter to an attorney who she says advised her that I was going to take our son from her if she did not file for divorce and claim domestic violence against me. She took many of the incidents that occurred that looked bad on her and superimposed them on me and made up a series of other lies to attempt to keep our son from me.
It worked for about 6 months and cost me nearly $100,000 in legal fees to get unsupervised visits reinstated with my son. I now have him 10 weeks a year, mostly in the summer. He has developed many of her traits with outbursts, signs of anger, and a terrible habit of lying and exaggerating.

Battered Secrets: *MEN* of Domestic Violence

My personal nightmare is much better, but in order to obtain my sanity with the courts with the way they are, my son is now the one who suffers.

In homes where domestic violence occurs, children are at high risk of suffering physical abuse themselves. Regardless of whether children are physically abused, the emotional effects of witnessing domestic violence are very similar to the psychological trauma associated with being a victim of child abuse. Each year, an estimated 3.3 million children witness domestic violence. -From Domestic Violence – A Guide for Health Care Professionals, State of New Jersey, Department of Community Affairs, March 1990.

Elva "Precious Love" Thompson

Chapter *III*

Jerry Miranda – USAF Academy, CO
Airfield Manager
Divorced

The much-publicized and televised show, 20/20 interview regarding the 25-year thrash with domestic violence victim, Jerry Miranda, saw the flare of a 10-inch blade that coiled into his back at his place of employment by his wife on the morning of May 5, 1999. With the helping hands of a co-worker, Jesse Howard, he threw himself at Mr. Miranda's wife, seizing the knife, awaiting police arrival. "They can't hold me forever. I'm going to come back and kill all of you!" A believable threat. In 2001, a judge ruled for 10 years in prison whereas Jerry thought that meant exactly 10 years, but Hassania Miranda had a different agenda. In 2002, Jerry's homicidal wife asked the judge for a reduction in her sentence to four years. She then applied to community corrections in 2003 and went before the parole board, but each time, they were unsuccessful attempts. Since then, there have been letters of protest from Jerry's co-workers out of fear that Hassania Miranda will make good on her promise.

Battered Secrets: *MEN* of Domestic Violence

The first time she had ever struck Jerry; he forgave her and stayed because he didn't want to put the family through a divorce. He was also in fear of his life because she threatened to kill him if he ever left her. No one ever knew, not even close relatives that there had been abuse in the marriage. It was a secret until Hassania Miranda showed up at her old house and pointed a gun at her son's friend. No explanation of why she did this, but the young man fled and Hassania posted bullets throughout the house as a calling card. She was arrested that night, posted bond and hours later, was released. The next morning, she phoned her husband's office and spoke with Jesse Howard and stated, "they took my gun, but it's okay...I have four more." Jesse pleaded with her to not do anything stupid, but what she did later that day, made Jesse a victim as well. Hassania Miranda's petition for sovereignty took place in Classroom No. 4 at the Pueblo Minimum Center.

Vice Chairman of the Colorado Board of Parole, Curtis Devin sat at the desk and the three men sat in front of him, Jerry Miranda, Jesse Howard, and one of their sons, Joe Miranda. Hassania Miranda walks in not making any eye contact with anyone. Joe Miranda moved his chair back away from his estranged mother, as it was the closest he had been to her without supervision from an armed officer in five years. Devin began to question Hassania Miranda about her

Elva "Precious Love" Thompson

drinking habits and if she recalled what brought her to this point. "A little," spoke the heavily accented Morocco voice. She and Jerry met in Athens, Greece when he was stationed in the Air Force there. Why do you think you would make a good parole candidate asked Devin. "Um," she replied, "I'm sober. I'm off my medication. I've learned a lot of things. I know why I did this, I hid behind a lot of things...watching TV, drinking." She said she drank because of the worry her two sons caused her. "I sit in the window, wait for them to come. I cry," she said. "I never sleep. I drink, drink." "I understand some of my problems better, if they let me out, I wouldn't bother anyone." She continued, "I been told by judge: If I go cross him, I go back to prison," she said. "That's why I don't." As Jerry Miranda listened with eager intention, he couldn't believe that he stayed married to her for 25 years.

Hassania Miranda was telling Devin how faithfully she attends her classes and how much her English has greatly improved. Her caseworker vouched for her. She was a good prisoner and good prisoners can earn days off their sentences, as many as 10 days a month until those days add up to 25 percent of their sentence. So far, Hassania has earned one year and 10 days.

Battered Secrets: *MEN* of Domestic Violence

Now, it was their turn. "She isn't sorry!" blurted Joe Miranda. She never apologized. She had gone to prison for stabbing Jerry, but she would hurt her sons many times too. She kicked Joe down the stairs and chased him with a knife. Next, was the relative who wanted to see her released, John Miranda, a son of Hassania's, not related to Jerry. "I personally think she does need to get out of here," John Miranda stated. "I'll make sure she is doing what she needs to do." Hassania gave him a smile. Jerry Miranda spoke up commenting, "my life has been miserable. Imagine going back to work and facing co-workers. Imagine everyone talking about you." Others thought he was an embarrassment to the academy. Some wondered how he could let a woman victimize him.

Jerry Miranda felt like he lost face, but at the same time, the attacks gave him a voice. He kept thinking about women killed by their husbands and now forgotten and how his co-workers saved him. He felt like he was alive for many reasons. "Maybe I'm the dead person who's standing up for them," he said. "Hassania Miranda always regarded herself as the victim. I made you put a knife in my back? I made you chase the children around with a knife?" he said. Hassania stated that she did want to apologize to her son as she rose and took a step toward

Elva "Precious Love" Thompson

Joe. He scooted his chair backward, ducking his head as if she might hit him. Hassania began to cry. "I think that's the first time in my life I'm talking sober to them," she stated. "I know what I did is not good." Curtis Devin then made a decision later that afternoon: Parole denied. When asked Jerry Miranda how he felt about the decision he stated, "It will never be over."

Battered Secrets: *MEN* of Domestic Violence

RESEARCHED FACTS

"**The Risk of Serious Physical Injury from Assault by a Woman Intimate.** The National Violence Against Women Survey estimates that each year, 1,510,455 women **and 834,732 men** are victims of physical violence by an intimate. Re-examination of the NVAW survey data on the form of victimization suggests that of the 834,732 men assaulted by an intimate, 90,241 men will be knifed, 180,483 threatened by a knife, 360,965 hit with an object, 67,681 beaten up and 620,049 slapped or hit."

"**Domestic Violence in Washington: 25,473 Men a Year** Applying the National Violence Against Women Survey's national estimate of the annual rate of violence by an intimate to Washington suggests that each year 42,824 women **and 25,473 men** are victims of physical violence by an intimate. Re-examination of the NVAW survey data on the form of victimization and applying those results to Washington suggests that a knife will be used on 2,754 men, 5,508 will be threatened with a knife and 11,016 hit with an object."

Elva "Precious Love" Thompson

"**Domestic Violence as seen in an Inner-City Emergency Room** Men are victims of domestic violence as often as women according to a study involving 516 patients at the emergency department of Charity Hospital, New Orleans, La. Using the validated Index of Spousal Abuse, the researchers said 19% of the women patients and 20% of the men had experienced recent physical violence. They pointed out that some experts fear attention to domestic violence against men will de-emphasize the importance of services for women."

Battered Secrets: *MEN* of Domestic Violence

Chapter *IV*

Anthony S. – 59, Providence, RI
Account Executive
Married for 41 years / Divorce pending
2 Children

"What happened to my sweet little wife?" stated Anthony, a 5 foot, 8 inch, 59-year-old account executive outside Providence, Rhode Island. **As I looked into the eyes of this distinguished firm speaking gentleman, I looked beyond the exterior and began to notice how he would fade out while acquainting me with his story. He seemed to be a bit embarrassed, but continued on with:**

My wife and I met back in 1967 at a carnival when we were young teenagers just graduating from high school. We weren't high school sweethearts at all, but we dated shortly after. A year later, we married and I obtained my accounting degree. "Sara" was a working woman. I was brought up in a family where the men were to "bring home the bacon." So you can imagine where we began to bump heads. Over the years, Sara joked about violence and how she could hit me if I made her angry enough, then she would always laugh

Elva "Precious Love" Thompson

afterwards and tell me" oh, but I'm only kidding." But one day, her jokes became taunts and threats. I was a working man and she felt the need to have a job outside of the house. I explained to her that I made enough money to support the both of us and our children and I did. There was no reason for her to get an outside job. She grew enraged and possessive of "her" things after that conversation. She started throwing tantrums over the littlest things. If the dishes weren't done correctly or if the trash wasn't taken out, I heard about it.

She would make little comments such as "I COULD KILL YOU!" or "YOUR THE ONE WITH THE JOB AND THE RESPONSIBILITIES, DO SOMETHING WITH YOURSELF!" Then one Saturday evening, we were preparing for a neighborhood cookout. We were in the kitchen and she asked me in a sweet sounding voice, "where's the ice?" I replied, "Oops! I forgot to pick it up from the market." I turned back around thinking it wasn't that big of a deal. Shortly after I turned, I felt sharp pain on the left side of my back. I reached my hand over my shoulder blade and I felt a warm liquid. I was bleeding. I turned completely around to find out what happened, and there she was, my wife, holding a fork in her hand with my blood on the blades.

Battered Secrets: *MEN* of Domestic Violence

What went through your mind at that moment... I was in total shock and disbelief. I just knew my wife couldn't have done this to me. I was at a loss for words. She stared me down with the coldest glare in her eyes. I've been married to this woman for 41 years, but this creature standing in my kitchen wasn't my wife. This was a demon in the form of the woman I woke up next to this morning. She threw the fork into the sink, ran the water, and exited the kitchen as if it was an accident of some sort. This type of behavior continued throughout the remainder of our marriage. I never called the police. She would hit me with the nearest object to her if I offended her in anyway. Instead of coming home to "hello honey, how was your day?" I was greeted by confrontations and usually broomsticks or lampshades.

They seemed to be the weaponry of choice for cleaning these days and I came home too late to participate in. The last straw was the evening she hit me in front of our children. We were sitting at the dinner table and I asked her to pass me the biscuits. She began throwing them at me one by one. At the time, our kids were over for dinner and they weren't quite sure how to react to this type of conduct coming from their mother.

Elva "Precious Love" Thompson

After all the biscuits were on the carpet next to my chair, she threw the bowl at me. She then got up and began punching me in my head and scratching my face. Our kids intervened and tried to stop her by pulling and tugging on their mothers' clothing shouting, "Mom no, please stop!" It was as if she was immune to her own children's cries because she would not let up. She began to hit me harder and dig her fingernails into my skin. My youngest son called the police. I grabbed her arms and thrust her up against the wall. She yelled for my daughter to call the police. Little did she know they already called the police, ON HER! When the police arrived, the kids explained to them in shock of what took place. I wanted to cry so badly for my kids because I never told them nor have they ever seen their mother strike me.

How are you feeling right now...I feel like we will never see our 50th wedding anniversary and my family are ultimately torn apart. Although my kids are grown, the sight of their mother acting in such a rage will forever be embedded in their minds. I filed for divorce, which is now pending and my sweet little Sara is now in jail for domestic abuse.

Chapter V

Jason R. – 27, Jacksonville, FL
Entrepreneur
Married for 4 years
No children

"If she left me, I wouldn't know what to do." Unlike most men, I had warnings signs. Michelle and I met in Junior college. She was (in my opinion) the most beautiful woman I've ever seen. The way her long black would wave at you when she walked away. I fell for her hard, and fast. We got married right out of college. I felt it was the right time for us to commit to each other. I could always tell she had doubts but I made myself believe that once she found out we were meant for each other, she would be sure of her decision to make me her husband. Things became rocky after about 3 years into the marriage. She began to drink heavy. I expressed to her my concern for her well-being. She told me I had a place in her life as her husband (putting emphasis on the word "husband") not her father. She told me she could do whatever she pleased. I didn't want to fight fire with fire by matching her level of intensity so I began to cry to her and plead for her to cut back on her drinking before it became a serious problem. She began to cry. She embraced me and promised me she would stop. This loving gesture went on for about 5 to 6 months. Then I began 2 find beer tops and cans around the bedroom. I would throw them away using trickery to make myself believe they were mine from the night before and I had just forgotten to pick them up. But, deep down, I knew they were Michelle's.

One day, I was looking for my work tie. I frantically searched the entire bedroom. I looked behind our dresser mirror and to my surprise there were about 30 beer cans and bottles stacked up. Some were empty, some where full; all I knew for sure was that I couldn't trick myself anymore. These weren't mine and it was time for me to do something. I called Michelle into the bedroom and I asked her what all the liquor behind the mirror was about. She replied, "Why are you asking me this? Do you think I'm sort of alcoholic? You think I'm crazy, don't you?" I didn't know how to react to her sudden outburst of psychotic anger. But, before I could think of what to do, she punched me in my stomach. I bent over to from the pain and she kneed me in my mouth. I looked down to the carpet to see a puddle of blood. I got up and ran to the bathroom. My mouth was dark red. I couldn't find a spot in my mouth that wasn't red. I came back into the bedroom and she was viciously pulling her things out of the closet and throwing them into a duffle bag that I've never seen before. I asked her where she thought she was going. Her response was "Somewhere you can't find me!" I didn't want her to leave, so grabbed the bag from her in a sad attempt to "put my foot down". She snatched it back and ran out the door and all I could do was breakdown and cry.

The next day, I received a call from her sister, asking me what I had done to Michelle. I retorted, "Not a thing. I confronted her drinking problem and she hit me." Her sister responded, "If she hit you, then what happened to her lip?" I honestly had no idea what she was talking about. So, unwisely I replied, "I don't know," because I really didn't. She hung up on me. About 3 hours later, Michelle called me. "I understand that you're upset about my drinking," she said, "but did you have to hit me?" Everything was making sense now. "Are you serious?" I said, "I NEVER put my hands on you and you know that." She began to cry, and apologize for her actions the night before. She said she needed me and she wanted to come home. We agreed to try again under a "no drinking" condition. When she arrived at the house the next day, her lip was busted. I poured herself into the house reeking of Jagermeister and Jack Daniels. I asked her to tell me what happened to her lip and she turned around slowly and replied, "You did this to me." At that moment, I knew my wife was crazy.

Realizing letting her back in the house was a huge mistake. I reached for the telephone and she stumbled into the kitchen and snatched it from me. She proceeded to hit me with the telephone and she then threatened to kill herself with the cord. I managed to get the phone away from her long enough to dial 911. She snatched it again, hung up it up, went into our bedroom, and actually tried to go to sleep. I didn't know what to do. I was stunned that alcohol can turn someone into such a different person. The police arrived and I showed them my scars and to make a long story short, they came into the house and apprehended her. My wife is now serving a year in prison with 5 years probation.

I know your going to think I'm crazy for this, but I decided to stay with my wife. I love her and I want to help her with her drinking problem. I am no one to judge, so for all of you that may want to judge me, refer to your "good book" *let he who is without sin...*

Chapter _VI_

Christopher S. – 20, Atlanta, GA
Full-time college student
Single
No children

"We were in love most of the time." Tyler and I met our freshman year in high school. It wasn't until our junior year that we came out to each other that we were both gay. We had become best friends, but we both knew we wanted it to be more. I had already come out to my parents the same day I came out to him, but Tyler's parents were strict Christians and we both knew they would have a tough time accepting him as a homosexual if not disowning him. So he asked me help him come out to his parents. He invited me over one day while his family was having dinner. We were all eating and Tyler grabbed my hand to let me know that he was about to spill the beans. I gave him a head nod to let him know that I was still here for him. He boldly looked up at his father and said, "Dad, I'm gay." His father replied through muffled laughing, "Sit down Tyler, I'm trying to finish my food." Tyler retorted, "I'm not kidding, I'm gay and I love Chris." His father knew he was serious. He looked up at Tyler, and then his eyes trailed towards me. He threw his plate at the wall, and he punched Tyler. He yelled for Tyler to get out of his house and to take his "faggot" friend with him. I was offended, but I was more worried for Tyler than anything. I was living alone so naturally, I told Tyler to get his things and to come stay with me. He did so and our relationship took off from there. We were so happy together.

When I was around him, I felt like I had to be better. Tyler had been through so much and the way he pulled through everything made me love him more. He was the bread winner and I took care of the house that quickly became "Our Home."; maybe too quickly because I grew very comfortable in my new life with him instantly. Tyler did too, but sometimes, he would stay out really late. I didn't want to give him a "curfew" so to speak, but I also didn't want him out all hours of the night. One evening, he came into the house at 6AM. I didn't know what to think or say. So I just threw on my robe and made him some coffee. I asked him where he was and he didn't answer me. He just went into the bedroom. I followed him and repeated my question. Tyler turned around and like lightening he slapped me right across my face. I fell to the ground by complete fright. He knelt down by myself and helped me get on the bed. He apologized repeated that night and he assured me it would never

Battered Secrets: _MEN_ of Domestic Violence

happen again. I believed him, after all never happened before. He kept his promise for 1 week exactly.

That following Thursday, he came home at 6AM again, but this time, I stayed in bed. When he climbed into bed, I asked him where he was and he calmly reached over and began to choke me. I begged for him to stop with the little strength I had. After he realized that my face was turning blue, he finally stopped and slept on the couch. The next morning, he left the house without a word. He came home and acted like nothing happened. I was wondering why every Thursday he had these random outbursts of violence. So, one Thursday, I followed him and to my surprise, he was going to the gay clubs downtown and staying out all night and morning with other men drinking God knows what else. I didn't say anything when he came that night when he came home. The next day, he took me out to McDonald's. We ate in and I thought it was the perfect time to confront him about his about his nights out. I asked, "Where do you go on Thursdays?", "Out." He replied. I repeated my questions. He retorted, "Don't do this here, not now." I grew upset and frustrated so I stood up and asked loudly, "WHERE DO YOU GO ON THURSDAYS?" He stood up and choked me until I fell to my knees.

Elva "Precious Love" Thompson

A bystander in the McDonald's called the police and I pleaded for them not to take him to jail. I didn't want him to get arrested. I just wanted to know the truth. I spoke to my mother on the phone and she explained to me that I did not need someone in my life if they were going to be putting their hands on me at anytime. She was so right. The police arrived and took Tyler to jail. I pressed charges and never looked back. Of course, I felt stupid and embarrassed. How could I have allowed something like that to happen? I should have left the first time, but I thought that he would change when he saw that I was willing to stick it out with him.

After some hard thinking and rebuilding of strength, I taught myself that I am worth more than that. I pulled myself together and managed to walk away from it all. I deserved better than what I was given. I decided to take time out for myself, to myself and work on me. **Christopher has since buried himself into his studies and has sworn off dating anyone until he received his Doctoral Degree in Psychology at Clark Atlanta University.**

Battered Secrets: *MEN* of Domestic Violence

Chapter *VII*

Brian C. – 36, Modesto, CA
HVAC installer
Married 16 years
1 child

December 11, 2009, the police pulled up to my home per my 911 call. I called begging for assistance because my wife was trying to kill me. When they arrived, guns were drawn and they demanded me to turn around with my hands in the air. I did what they asked at the same time trying to explain why I called, but before I could say anything, they ordered me to "shut up" and started roughly handcuffing me. My 82-year-old grandmother came outside at that time and yelled to the officers that my wife was trying to kill me. She told them to take my wife to jail and to let me go, but they didn't pay my grandmother any mind. The one female officer walked over to my grandmother, shushing her, walking her back inside the house. I caught a glimpse of my wife standing on the porch as if nothing happened. She was just holding our son in her arms looking at me as if I had done something to her. She even shed a few tears. Needless to say, they believed her instead of me. Guess it was the tears. It

Elva "Precious Love" Thompson

didn't seem to matter that I was bleeding on my arm from the knife cut she managed to jab at me. She didn't have a scratch on her, but nobody thought that to be strange in the least accept for my grandmother and me. **With the sound of quivering in his voice, Brian sound as if he was trying to hold back tears, as he reminisced of his trying passage.**

It all started from an argument about our son. JoAnne was sitting in the living room watching TV when I came home from being on call with my job. When I walked in the door, I immediately noticed my son crying and screaming. I asked what was wrong and she said without looking at me that "me-maw" was tending to the baby. I walked in my son's room and there was my grandmother holding my little boy in her arms, unable to comfort him in a way where he would stop crying. We are talking about an 82-year-old woman here trying to calm a crying 18-month-old baby. For the life of me, I couldn't figure out why my wife would allow this to happen. She didn't even try to help my grandmother. She just sat on the couch as if she had earplugs. I relieved my grandmother by taking my son into my arms, trying to talk to him to calm him down, letting him know that Daddy was here. I gave him a bottle, which seemed to help for the most part and laid my son down and turned on his overhead mobile to help calm him.

After making sure he was okay, I shut his door around and I started yelling at JoAnne asking her what the hell her problem was. She jumped up and lashed out at me and started screaming that she has to do "everything" around here and how tired she is of being maid, mom, and wife. She was acting like a crazy woman! She started throwing couch pillows at me to picture frames, and vases. It was total chaos. She told me how much she hated me and how she didn't want to move here to California in the first place. She was just out of control. The look in her eyes was weird. It was like she was a different person. My wife used to be sweet and happy-go-lucky. I didn't know what was going on with her lately.

Where there ever any signs that maybe something was going wrong somewhere in your marriage or changes in your wife's personality? Thinking back, I did start to notice after I would get home from work, the smell of dirty diapers as soon as I hit the front door and the house would be a mess, not to mention my wife would be a mess too. Her hair was always in disarray and she stayed in her bathrobe all the time. No dinner would be made. I would have to make myself a sandwich or hit up a fast food restaurant just before I got home. It was ridiculous. I hated that my marriage was turning out like this, especially with my son being in this world. My parents never did approve of our marriage anyway, but I thought that by moving, it would ease some tension. Seems like it only made things worse, but I never thought it would be to this extent. She just seemed so uptight lately. If I would say something she didn't like, she would punch me on the arm repeatedly at her hardest with her teeth clinched cursing me out. She would even do this in front of our son and my grandmother. I wouldn't hit her back, but I would try to restrain her by holding her arms, but that made her even madder and she would start kicking me, aiming for my manhood and even resorted to spitting in my face because I refused to let her arms go. I didn't want her to hit me anymore. I just wanted peace and for her to be okay.

It was our anniversary and I decided to take JoAnne out for dinner. I arranged for a baby-sitter to come to the house so there wouldn't much pressure on my grandmother, which I thought was a good idea. We got into the car, and as we were on our way to the restaurant, out of nowhere, JoAnne starts going on a rampage. She started punching me, full force in my face like I was a punching bag and scratching me. We started to swerve on the road, so I had to pull over. I got out of the car and asked her where all of this was coming from. She said that she didn't even want to go out and why did we have to leave our son with my "witch" of a grandmother. I explained to her that I hired a babysitter to help grandmother, and then she started accusing me of sleeping with the baby-sitter. She is a young teenaged girl and I have never cheated on my wife. I didn't know where all of this was coming from.

I mean, here I was doing something nice for our anniversary and she was being ungrateful. I just walked away to get back in the car when she picks up a large stick from the ground and starts beating me with it. The pain was excruciating. I fell to the ground and put my hands up to cover my head yelling her name demanding for her to stop. My hands had scratches from the bark of the tree and my head had a few cuts and scrapes. Then my sweet little wife gets into the car and drives off. I was left to take a cab back home.

What went through your mind at that moment…Well, to be honest, I wanted to pay her back some kind of way. I wanted her to hurt the way she has hurt me. I was livid.

Elva "Precious Love" Thompson

My mind could not process the actual event. That had to be the worse thing that has happened in our marriage. She was certainly not the woman I married 16 years ago. She is just not the same woman at all. What makes me angrier is the fact that I still love her. **Brian then asked me, "How does that happen?" "How do you continue to love someone that physically harms you?" "How do you deal with it?" I briefed Brian with a little about my past of being in an abusive marriage. I shared that it wasn't easy, but he had to adjust his thinking and focus on his child's welfare, as well as himself...silence took over our conversation. I asked Brian if he was okay. After a 7 second pause, he cleared his throat.** I was married to JoAnne for 16 years and I thought I knew her, but apparently, I don't. It's heartbreaking. I feel like the gods are punishing me for something. I know she has issues but maybe we can go to counseling. I don't want to just throw away 16 years and break up my family. Maybe if we go to counseling, she will change. When she sees that I still want our marriage to work, she will change back to the woman I fell in love with many years ago.

Brian began to justify why he decided to stay... All of our years together weren't bad, just some of the years, but not all. With

Battered Secrets: *MEN* of Domestic Violence

marital counseling, I know that we will be okay. I just can't let go...my son needs his mother.

In doing research, I found that men stay in abusive relationships / marriages for the protection of their children. Afraid that if they leave, they will never be allowed to have contact with their child(ren) or that he would be labeled as a "bad dad" by the mother. They also assume blame and feel liable by thinking that they can do something that will "make it all better." Then the feelings of melancholy or anxiety set in.

It is a common theory that women are abuse victims and men are always the abusers. There are numerous rationales of why the community believes men are in no way sufferers and why women often disregard the likelihood. Domestic violence against men have been diminished, substantiated, and neglected for a very long time. Little consideration has been paid to the subject of domestic abuse / violence against males, mainly because violence against women has been evident and was overlooked for so long.

Elva "Precious Love" Thompson

Chapter *VIII*

James A. – 43, Scottsdale, AZ
CEO (Business Owner)
Married 23 years

While married to my wife for 23 years, 19 of them was verbal abuse along with mental anxiety. The physical abuse was throughout our marriage with punches here and there or slaps by my wife, seems like little things about me would piss her off. As much as I wanted to, I would never hit her back. I love her, but sometimes, she would drive me to that point, but I could never hit her. **What reaction would you have towards your wife whenever she felt compelled to strike you?** I would try to restrain her by catching her hands or try to hold her arms. I recall once when I held her arms to keep her from slapping me, she spit in my face and verbally abused me with calling me all kinds of choice words I can't even bring myself to repeat right now. I mean, she would really tear into me with curse words I never even heard of or thought she knew. **With a look of gloom on James' face and swelling of his eyes, his voice tone lowered…**I just can't believe it. I mean whatever happened to love, honor, and obey? It

Battered Secrets: *MEN* of Domestic Violence

seems like she lost respect for me and I have done nothing but provide for her. I made sure she had everything she wanted and made sure she lived a comfortable lifestyle. I know the type of life she lived before we met from her ex-spouse and I'm sure he was a hard-working fella, but he couldn't give her what I have given her. Her happiness was all that mattered to me and I wanted her to have nothing but the best. **Was there ever a time when you said enough was enough and thought to call the police?** Many times I felt like that and did at one point go to the authorities, but I didn't get much help. I actually went to the police station to talk to somebody and an officer came out to talk to me. I began explaining to him what was going on in my household and when I began telling him that I wished to file a report against my wife, he cut me off, trying to cover up smirks and hold back chuckles asking me, "Are you sure you want to do this Sir?" I just stared at him, got up, and walked out. I got no help whatsoever. Talk about embarrassment and humiliation. I didn't even want to go home. I drove to my office and sat at my desk with my Cohiba cigar and my gal pal Brandy...*a glass of Christian Brothers Brandy* and drowned myself in my sorrow. I didn't make it home that night. The most relaxation I've had in years.

Elva "Precious Love" Thompson

I must have been asleep all night because I was awoken by loud screams and shattering glass and when I looked up, there was my wife hovering over me with my Louisville slugger. She managed to pound me in the head and back a few times before security grabbed hold of her. I was devastated. My secretary called the police as a few of my employees tried to help security hold my wife down and retrieve the bat. She was yelling and screaming that I was a cheater, but I never cheated on my wife all the time we were married and even when we were courting. I love her in spite of. Well, the police arrived and my employees were pointing at my wife for them to take her. I was embarrassed, humiliated, and devastated all at once. Everyone thought that my household was in order. I portrayed it to be anything but. Now I had to explain that I was a battered spouse at the age of 43.

Are you and your spouse still married or are you going to file for a divorce? I filed for a divorce, which is pending. I have had enough. I always knew she was crazy, but I never thought she would go to this extreme and actually show up at my place of business in this manner. I did file a police report. She is now the property of the State of Arizona. I still love her. I was married to her for 23 years, but I cannot go through another 23 years living the way we have been living. I love her, but I don't want to see her again, although I had to show up at trial. A few of my employees came with me for moral support and to be witnesses. When my wife saw me take the stand, she had the audacity to threaten me right in front of the judge by saying that she was going to "kill me!" She even tried to come at me, but was restrained by the deputies. The judge didn't even listen to my story, he just sentenced her right then and there and gave her a 5 year sentence along with counseling, of which is much needed, but I think 5 years was a slap on the wrist, especially with threatening to kill me in front of a judge.

How are you feeling right now? It hurts you know. I feel like I lost a little piece of me. I mean, I know what she has done throughout our marriage, but it didn't stop me from loving her, but enough was enough you know. I have my brother, who has been there for me throughout it all and my employees give me great support. I'm just sorry to them that they had to witness what they witnessed. I myself will be attending counseling just to make sure that I am all right. This book helps too and I thank you for writing something like this for fellas like me. This is much needed.

Elva "Precious Love" Thompson

Although James didn't want to go too much into detail of all the events that took place throughout his marriage, I still thank him for his participation. I have great faith and belief that he will get through this with his loving support system. All the best to James.

Very little is known about the actual number of men who are in a domestic relationship in which they are abused or treated violently by women. In 100 domestic violence situations, approximately 40 cases involve violence by women against men. An estimated 400,000 women per year are abused or treated violently in the United States by their spouse or intimate partner. This means that roughly 300,000 to 400,000 men are treated violently by their wife or girlfriend. (www.antimisandry.com)

Domestic violence against men is an all too real issue that doesn't get as much attention as it should. There are an overwhelming number of domestic violence statistical data illustrating domestic violence against women. But, there is also plenty of evidence of men being subjected to domestic violence as well. Some statistics suggest that out of every 100 reported domestic violence cases, about 40 of them are against men. (www.articlebase.com)

Battered Secrets: *MEN* of Domestic Violence

Chapter *IX*

Michael B. – 17, Philadelphia, PA
High School Student

Amelia and I started dating in October 2006. We kept it a secret because her mom didn't allow her to date and my mom didn't care for interracial couples. Being in school and sharing some of the same classes was the most that we would see each other. I mean we would sneak around town and lie to our parents and say that we were going to a friend's house, of which we would actually go, but the other would be there. **How long did you date before the abuse began?** It was like 2 weeks. She slapped me for something that I said and apparently, she didn't like. I thought it was funny, but she didn't. I can't even remember what I said, that's how so unimportant it was. When she slapped me, at first, I thought she was playing, but she kept slapping left and right and right and left on each side of my face. I knew then that she was serious and I stopped her by grabbing her arms and pushing her away from me. We were over our friend's house and when they saw me push her away, they stepped in between us because she was coming after me still. I didn't want to hit this girl, but I wasn't going to let her keep hitting me either. Especially in front of our friends, but that didn't stop her from continuing to put her hands on me. She was so violent and would say mean things to me like she "hated me" and "was only with me for sympathy." **How did that make you feel to hear those things?** She really hurt my feelings, especially the sympathy part when she knew about my situation with my mom and step dad of he and I didn't get along and my mom was always taking his side. She would always use that as a weapon and call me a wimp and a punk.

There was an incident where she pushed my head up against the garage door because I left my bike on the side of her house. We didn't live that far from each other so I thought it was okay to leave it there, but she didn't think it was a good idea because like I said before, her mom was strict about our dating and she thought I was being careless. **How do your friends feel about your relationship with Amelia? Do they know about other incidents or did they just witness that one?** The incident that one time in front of our friends was the only time they witnessed anything. Other than that, I never told anyone about what was going on. For the most part, I was afraid that I would get laughed at by my friends and I didn't want to be embarrassed. She would hit me out of anger about stuff that I didn't do, but she was just mad at the time and it could have been something that went on in her household. She would take it out on me.

Amelia always took stuff out on me. She would call me names all the time and say that I was stupid and that I was never going to be anything. Her words cut deep, but I tried to not show it, especially when I was around my friends. I would play it off in front of them like our relationship was great. I would always say that we were good whenever my friends would ask about us.

It was hard carrying on a relationship with Amelia. It was hard for me to concentrate on school too because in my head, all I would hear was Amelia's voice telling me how stupid I was and how I was never gonna be nothing. My grades started dropping from Bs and Cs to Fs. I started skipping school a lot too. Whenever I skipped school, she would really get upset with me because she was always accusing me of another girl, so quite naturally, she thought that I was skipping with a girl, but I would actually be with my friends and go smoking and drinking. I didn't care much about myself anymore. I already had it bad at home and then my girlfriend would tear me down. I was feeling so bad that I started to believe that I was those things that

Elva "Precious Love" Thompson

Amelia kept calling me. It got to the point where I wouldn't show up to school at all except to catch the bus with Amelia after school was over.

When I would get on the bus with her, she would cut her eyes at me so tuff. If looks could kill, I would have been dead many times before. After the bus drop off, I would walk her half way home, but she continued on with tearing me down and slapping me around. She did it so much that she gave me a purple eye. Not a black eye, but a purple eye. I told my mom that I got into a fight at school. **Was there ever a time that you thought about breaking up with her because of her violent behavior?** Yes! Absolutely, but I still cared about her and that made it hard until she did something so bad that really made me walk away from her for good. **What did she do?** She tore me down in front of our friends and started slapping me around again and punching me in the face all while yelling at me, calling me names of "your worthless" and saying that I wasn't "shit" all because we were over one of our friends house who had a costume party, it was Halloween and I was waiting for her to come and when she did, she saw me talking to another girl that I knew since grade school, but Amelia didn't know that part and she didn't care either. When she walked in and saw me talking, she screamed at my friend telling her

Battered Secrets: *MEN* of Domestic Violence

to stay away from me or she was going to kill her, then she looked at me and hit me over the head with a glass. There was blood everywhere. I had deep cuts on top of my head and on my face. The parents of the kid's party kicked Amelia out of the house and called the police. It was a huge mess. By this time, both our families knew then that we were seeing each other.

The police arrived and the parents had already called my mom and step dad and they pressed charges. Amelia went to jail that night and I went to the hospital where I got 23 stitches across my head and 11 stitches on my face. She was charged with assault with a deadly weapon and was given 6 months in jail and 5 years probation and counseling. My mom sent me back to Philly to be with my real dad, which wasn't much better, but this was my mom's way of keeping me away from Amelia.

It's been almost a year now and I heard she had a new boyfriend that she was doing the same thing to. I'm glad that I'm away from her, but I hate that I still care for her.........

Elva "Precious Love" Thompson

Teenagers often experience violence in dating relationships. <u>Statistics</u> show that one in three teenagers has experienced violence in a dating relationship. In dating violence, one partner tries to maintain <u>power and control</u> over the other through abuse. Dating violence crosses all racial, economic and social lines. Most victims are young women, who are also at greater risk for serious injury. Young women need a <u>dating safety plan</u>. (www.acadv.org).

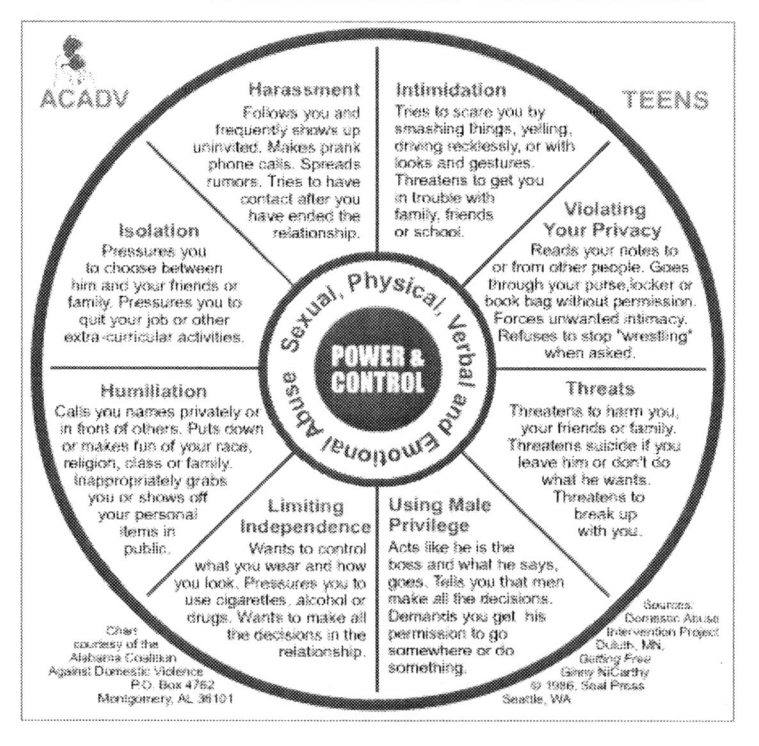

Teenage violence linked to later domestic violence. Adolescents who engaged in violent behavior at a relatively steady rate through their

Battered Secrets: *MEN* of Domestic Violence

teenage years and those whose violence began in their mid teens and increased over the years are significantly more likely to engage in domestic violence in their mid 20s than other young adults. – (www.ScienceDaily.com)

Elva "Precious Love" Thompson

Chapter *X*

Marshawn H. – 21, Atlanta, GA
Junior – Major: Engineering
Georgia State University
Defensive Running Back

I could see that Marshawn was nervous and he looked to be a little embarrassed, but I tried to make him feel as relaxed and comfortable as I possibly could. Over lunch at a local restaurant, he began to take it easy and open up to me more. No one would ever think that I would be hiding something like this. I mean, I'm an athlete and a damn good one too! I can't believe I'm talking about this with you, but I must admit, it feels good to let it out, kind of like therapy. I never liked therapists though. Anytime a man needs to talk about his feelings on a couch you know something's wrong. Where do I start with my ex-girlfriend? Celeste was a very nice girl in the beginning. She came across extremely sweet and intelligent. However, there was a dark side to Celeste that no one knew about. She allowed this side to show when she was intoxicated and/or angry with me or any old thing. The very first time I encountered her abuse was in the comfort of my dorm room. We were watching television

Battered Secrets: *MEN* of Domestic Violence

and I saw a female who was attractive on the show we were viewing. I made a comment about her looks and Celeste flipped out on me. She began by throwing pillows at me. I started throwing the pillows back in a joking-type manner. Celeste said, "Oh, so this is funny to you?" She then retaliated by punching me in my stomach and attempting to knee me in my groin. I got up and walked to the door at a fast pace with her jacket in my hand. She then followed me in a rage. I opened the door and politely showed her the way out. She snatched her jacket from me and slammed my door behind her. After a few exercise routines and some yoga for men, I made up in my mind that she was just playing too rough and she deserved another chance to redeem herself. I gave her a few days to cool off before I made the decision to give her a call. I loved her and I wasn't going to pretend that I didn't just because we had a little fight.

Like I said, I love Celeste, but there were times when she would get real upset and jealous over other females for nothing. I mean she would be in a rage where she felt like I was cheating on her when I never have. She was just so insecure. I always tried my best to make her happy, but when she doesn't get all of the attention, it's a problem. It would be such a problem to the point where she has dug her nails into my skin and I would have marks and scars on my arms, my neck, and my face. I would always tell the guys that I had a bad ass cat at home. I would never hit Celeste back because I was raised right by my mother and grandmother to never hit a female. I knew better. My folks would kick my ass if they ever heard about me putting my hands on a female. **What did your family think about your marks and scratches, did they ever inquire where they came from?** Yeah, but I would lie and tell them that I got scraped up in practice, but I think my grandmother knew I was lying. **Yeah, grandmothers always know don't they...so wise.**

A couple of my teammates would inquire also about my marks, but I would play it off by laughing and making a sexual gesture in regards to the marks. Celeste was no joke. She would probably be pissed right now if she knew we were out together. She's crazy like that you know, like the time when my little cousin came into town, our mom's are sisters. This is a cousin that Celeste has never met. My cousin, a couple of my guys, and myself all went to a sports bar downtown Atlanta and tell me why Celeste just happened to be downtown too, out with her girlfriends. Well, one of her girlfriends spotted my car with my cousin in the front seat. It was on from there. It was like a high speed chase. Celeste was acting crazy as hell.

Battered Secrets: *MEN* of Domestic Violence

While following me with speed behind my car, she called my cell phone and started screaming, wanting to know, in her words, "who is that bitch you got with you?!" "I'm gonna kick her ass, you better stop the fuckin' car now!" I pulled over to a nearby gas station and I couldn't even get out of the car good before she went on the passengers side of my car, opened the door, drug my little cousin out of the car, and started punching, slapping, and kicking her. My friends and I quickly grabbed hold of Celeste and I told her to get her hands off my cousin. With the look of wanting to kill in her eyes, she didn't believe me at first until I told her my cousin's name, of which she then remembered me talking about her and her mom coming to town from Virginia to visit.

It was terrible. That was a time when I wanted to put my hands on Celeste for hurting my little cousin the way she did. Talk about first impressions. **I can only imagine what went through your mind, especially your cousin to have this stranger attack her. What did you do?** I don't even want to get into all of that right now because it makes me even madder just thinking about it and my family is not feeling Celeste at all, but you know, it's ultimately my decision and even though that should have been the last straw for me with her, it wasn't. The last straw for me was when she and I had

Elva "Precious Love" Thompson

plans true enough, but practice went into overtime. The guys and I were in the locker room and she walked in, not caring that most of the guys were half naked and she just tore into me with her nails and started yelling and screaming about being late because she made reservations for dinner.

She was pissed because we were supposed to have dinner with her parents, but like I said, practice went into overtime, nothing I could do about it. She didn't want to hear that. When the guys saw her scratching me up, I was trying to restrain her and some of them thought it was funny while the others was trying to pull her away from me. I was too embarrassed in front of my people. I mean to see this girl with her little 5 foot frame no more than 100 pounds and here I am 5' 8" 190 and she getting the best of me. I just didn't want to put my hands on her. She got me good too. My face was scratched up, blood trickling. It was a bad scene. Right then, I let her go. I didn't want anything to do with her, but she keeps calling me and I keep pressing ignore.

It got so bad to the point where she was stalking me, showing up at practice, standing on the sidelines yelling

Battered Secrets: *MEN* of Domestic Violence

my name. My coach had to escort her from the area. She would drive by my mom's house blowing the horn late at night and even call my grandmother's house and hang up when she answered. The girl is crazy. I can't believe I dealt with her from the beginning, but she portrayed herself to be something different. She used to be so sweet. I guess you never know a person like you think you do. I ended up having to put a restraining order out on her. It doesn't stop her from calling me private. I know it's her, but it does stop her from coming around my family's house and my dorm.

Everyday is relief because I used to look over my shoulder. To be honest, I think she withdrew from school. She was always talking about going back to her hometown of North Carolina. As far as I'm concerned, she can go wherever. The next time I get involved with a young lady, I'm going to make sure to check out her history and her family. It's not always about looks. My grandmother taught me that one! *Marshawn and I completed our lunch and interview and as he was walking away, I thought about why men are less likely to call the police, even when there is plain visible evidence of abuse on their person. I think that maybe they feel ashamed, as women do who are also victims, however, for men, they have a shame complexed of not being able to control their girlfriends or spouses.*

Elva "Precious Love" Thompson

They believe a "real man" would be able to keep her managed. Additionally, law enforcement has a propensity to allocate these similar customary gender role expectations. This appends to the permissible und narrow opinion that the wrongdoer is a man. As a result, the law is disinclined to take women into custody for domestic assault.

Battered Secrets: *MEN* of Domestic Violence

STATISTICS

WWW.ABOUT.COM

Allen-Collinson, J. (2009). A marked man: Female perpetrated intimate partner abuse. International Journal of Men's Health, 8, (1), 22-40. (A case study of an abused heterosexual man. Article examines themes obtained from interviews and personal diary material.)

Ridley, C. A., & Feldman, C. M. (2003). Female domestic violence toward male partners: Exploring conflict responses and outcomes. Journal of Family Violence, 18 (3), 157-170. (Participants were 153 female volunteers who completed the Abusive Behavior Inventory. Results reveal that 67.3% of participants reported at least one occurrence of perpetrating violent behavior in the past year. Most frequent behaviors included pushing, shoving, holding down <45.1%> and slapping, hitting, biting <41.2%>.)

Shook, N. J., Gerrity, D. A., Jurich, J. & Segrist, A. E. (2000). Courtship violence among college students: A comparison of verbally *and physically abusive couples. Journal of Family Violence, 15, 1-22. (A modified Conflict Tactics Scale was administered to 572 college students <395 women; 177 men>. Results reveal that significantly more women than men, 23.5% vs 13.0%, admitted using physical force against a dating partner.)*

Bookwala, J., Frieze, I. H., Smith, C., & Ryan, K. (1992). Predictors of dating violence: A multi variate analysis. Violence and Victims, 7, 297-311. (Used CTS with 305 college students <227 women, 78 men> and found that 133 women and 43 men experienced violence in a current or recent dating relationship. Authors reports that "women reported the expression of as much or more violence in their relationships as men." While most violence in relationships appears to be mutual--36% reported by women, 38% by men-- women report initiating violence with non violent partners more frequently than men <22% vs 17%>).

A University of Pennsylvania emergency room report found 13% of men reported being assaulted by a female partner in the previous 12 months, of which 50% were choked, kicked, bitten, punched, or had an object thrown at them, 37% involved a weapon, and 14% required medical attention.

Battered Secrets: *MEN* of Domestic Violence

Why Women Assault:

California State University surveyed 1,000 college women: 30% admitted they assaulted a male partner. Their most common reasons: (1) my partner wasn't listening to me; (2) my partner wasn't being sensitive to my needs; and (3) I wished to gain my partner's attention.

University of Pennsylvania Professor Richard Gelles states: "Contrary to the claim that women only hit in self-defense, we found that women were as likely to initiate the violence as were men. In order to correct for a possible bias in reporting, we reexamined our data looking only at the self-reports of women. The women reported similar rates of female-to-male violence compared to male-to-female, and women also reported they were as likely to initiate the violence as were men," in his article reprinted at **The Hidden Side of Domestic Violence**

Elva "Precious Love" Thompson

A FEW WORDS FROM THE AUTHOR

Some researchers advocate that the intention for intimate partner aggression against men by women may hold opposing views from those for aggression against women by men, and that women endure more brutal grievance than men. However, the incidence of abuse by women against men and its effect, justify awareness. It is imperative for the sufferers of abuse, be it men or women, to discern that they are not alone and that such occurrence is not distinctive to their personal circumstances. It is also imperative for the perpetrators of intimate partner aggression (men and/or women) to distinguish that violence in any structure is both ethically and lawfully wrong.

- Survivor, Elva Thompson
www.preciousheartsfoundation.org

Battered Secrets: *MEN* of Domestic Violence

RESOURCES

Battered Men's Helpline: 1-877-643-1120 access code: 0757

ONLINE RESOURCES:

Men and Domestic Abuse

Family Violence Prevention Services http://www.serve.com/fvps/

S.A.F.E (Stop Abuse For Everyone) http://www.safe4all.org/

National Men's Center http://themenscenter.com/national.html

Support: http://familyofmen.com/

Domestic Abuse Defined: http://www.dvmen.org/dv-9.htm#pgfld-1000404

Domestic Abuse Helpline for Men and Women: http://www.dahmw.org

ABOUT THE AUTHOR

Elva Thompson is a 20-year veteran of the writing era economy, started out with spoken word/poetry that later ventured into short stories and blossomed into biographies and autobiographies for herself as well as others. She is available as a guest speaker against domestic violence, as well as to discuss her book publishing company, (Esquire Publications) www.esquirepublications.com and her editorial service, (Georgia Editing Service, LLC) www.georgiaeditingservice.com and her novels, which she refers to as her "ministry," as each book factors life changing experiences that was dealt with in a spiritual dominion.

This selfless woman of God is also an advocate for her affiliate, (DAHMW) *www.dahmw.org* where she is a helpline volunteer and operator. Elva is also President of her own nonprofit organization, (Precious Hearts Foundation Incorporation), *www.preciousheartsfoundation.org* an organization that will be an aid to all domestic abuse victims, as well as others that will provide shelter, meals, clothing, and eventually employment.

To contact Elva refer to: info@preciousheartsfoundation.org

Check out this domestic abuse survivor story
"A Mother's Cry"
Inspirational!

This book is an inspiring autobiography about a young woman who stayed in a fifteen-year abusive marriage for the sake of her three children when without notice, she finds herself filing for divorce on the grounds of abandonment because her husband walked out on her and their daughters. She then had to put her business on hold, moved her family to another state to start over where she tries to adjust to becoming a divorced, single parent. With being in a new state; she strives to get her business back together, the ups and downs of raising her children alone, and at the same time, going through the struggle of getting to know herself again. This book explores the victories and defeats of single parenthood, dating, and starting life over under new management.

Book Order Form
Please (√) your novel(s) of interest

Quantity	Title	Price
	Nonfiction – **"A Mother's Cry"**	$12.99 + $2.99 s/h
	Nonfiction – **"Love Jones, The Real Version"**	$12.99 + $2.99 s/h
	Nonfiction – **"Jailed By Blood: Inmate 798175 "**	$12.99 + $2.99 s/h
	Nonfiction – **"Memoirs of Cancer Survivors: AMERICA's Relay for Life"**	$12.99 + $2.99 s/h
	Nonfiction – **"Battered Secrets: MEN of Domestic Violence"**	$12.99 + $2.99 s/h
	Nonfiction – **"Heaven's Bouquet: Planted and Picked by God"**	$12.99 + $2.99 s/h

*Please allow 5-7 business days for mail in orders
**Sorry no personal checks accepted

Name: _____
Mailing Address: _____
City / State / Zip: _____
Telephone: _____
E-mail: _____

Make money orders and/or cashier's checks payable to:
Esquire Publications
c/o Elva Thompson
P. O. Box 241
Morrow, GA 30260
www.esquirepublications.com